JC

County Fair

Written and Photographed by
Steve Lesberg and Naomi Goldberg

COUNTY FAIR was photographed at the 88th Annual Southern California Exposition, Del Mar, California.
The publishers wish to express their gratitude to the following people without whose splendid cooperation this book would not be possible.
Southern California Exposition Board of Directors,
22nd District Agricultural Association:
R. R. Richardson, President
Frank Strauss, Vice President
Ernest Miller
Chaffey Young
Elaine Barnes
Arlene Straza
William Moeser
Charles E. Badger
Donald Thiel
William Dumond, General Manager
Public Relations Staff:
Bill Arballo, Director
Connie Geritz
Jo Jordan
Harry Hofmann
Ron Oakes
John McDonald
California Mid-Winter Fair, Imperial Valley, California:
Dick Montejano, General Manager
Bob Brown
Jim Duncan
and the countless others who assisted us throughout the project.

First Published 1978 by
Peebles Press International, Inc.
10 Columbus Circle, New York, New York 10019

Designed by Ann Louise Pepe

ISBN 0-672-52369-8
Library of Congress Catalog Card Number 77-75693

Distributed by
The Bobbs-Merrill Co., Inc.
4300 West 62nd St., Indianapolis, Indiana 46268, U.S.A.

Printed and bound in the United States of America

Introduction...

Every year, people the world over attend meetings to show off the fruits of their labor, to compare ideas, to gain valuable knowledge, and to have a grand old time. The occasion may be a world's fair, an industrial trade show, or a church bazaar. The location may be a large urban sports complex, thousands of square feet of convention hall space, or a rural shopping center parking lot. These gatherings are called "fairs". People go to fairs for a lot of reasons and they've been doing so for hundreds of years. Attendance figures and participation, in almost ever case, continue to grow.

An American county fair is an excellent example of this international phenomenon. Not only has its concept emerged from examples set by the rest of the world, but it has also developed its own qualitities that make it uniquely "American".

A county fair is normally held once a year, often in the same location. The length of time it remains open is determined by the number of exhibitors, the expected attendance, and by past experience. Traditionally, it is an agricultural exposition with emphasis on anything generated for or from the farm community. Modern county fairs have grown to encompass virtually any product or service generated within the county. They also continue to be a major influence on the success of such programs as the Future Farmers of America and 4-H Clubs as every year the cash awards are larger and the livestock auctions more crowded.

Although large amusement areas and big name entertainment are popular attractions, the emphasis always remains on county progress. For each person who comes to a fair to ride the double Ferris wheel, there is always someone who comes to view the new products and someone else who comes to see the livestock.

Visiting a fair is truly a unique experience. It is a feast for the senses, an opportunity to escape from the commonplace. It is a world filled with the aroma of fresh popcorn, the sounds of music and laughter, and a kaleidoscope of colors. Every step is an adventure. Whether you stay in a group or wander alone at your own pace, it is often impossible to see and do everything at a large fair in one day.

Let us take you through the main gate to a county fair. Whether it's your first visit or your fiftieth, you're in for a treat. You'll see well-known entertainers, you'll see local talent. You can buy a miracle mop from a professional pitchman and you can bid on a blue ribbon lamb raised by a local youngster. We'll take you to the rodeo and to the horse show. You'll see the start of the balloon race, the baked goods judging, the fireworks, and much more.

There is something for everyone here, so wear comfortable shoes and listen to the P.A. announcements for we don't want you to miss anything.

WELCOME
TO
OUR
FAIR

Good morning! We'd like to extend a cordial welcome to all fairgoers and invite you to enjoy the hundreds of things to see and do here at this our eighty-eighth annual county fair. It's a beautiful day and we expect record crowds, so if you should become separated from your group, here are some helpful hints: make a mental note of where your car is parked and establish a landmark on the grounds where all can meet.

Remember . . . the Lost Child Station is located at the rear of the Grandstand. There are also children's name tags, strollers, and wheelchairs available at the main gate.

We'll keep you advised as to the times and locations of most everything going on today, so keep listening and have a great time!

Grants
Hamburgers
Sandwiches

Connie, please return the white cart to the P.R. Office.

hon

arts

Local nimble-fingered knitters and seamstresses display their wares in our Clothing and Textile Exhibit at the Home Arts Building. . .

You will also see demonstrations and be able to ask questions of the exhibitors.

Butterflies & Moths of the

The theme of this year's Hobby Show is "Things That People Do". The show is also chock-full of photography, fine arts, and special-interest collections. The Hobby Show Building is located along the Midway across from the Trade Mart.

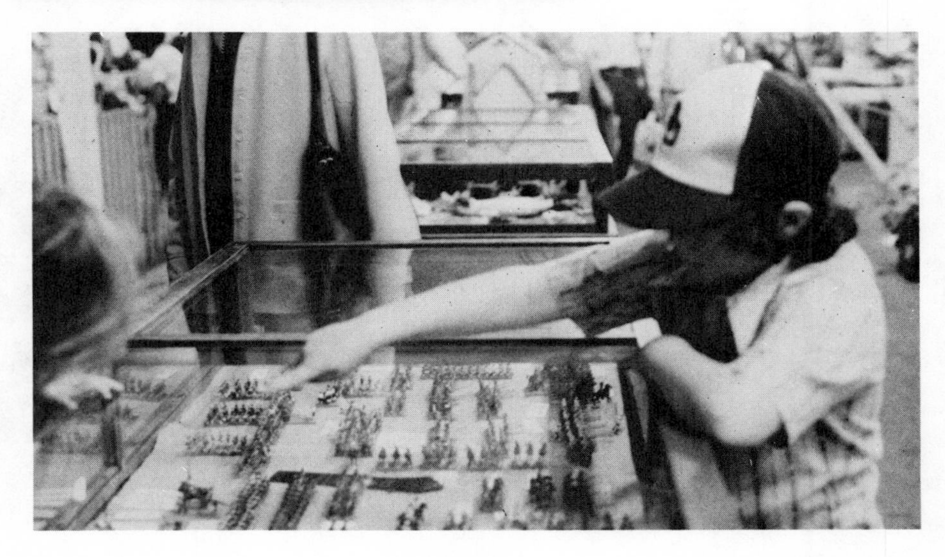

Touch My Leaves
See What Happens!

See the many varieties of locally cultivated plants in unusual landscaped settings at this year's outdoor Flower and Garden Show. It's more lush and colorful than ever before.

GEMS & MINERALS

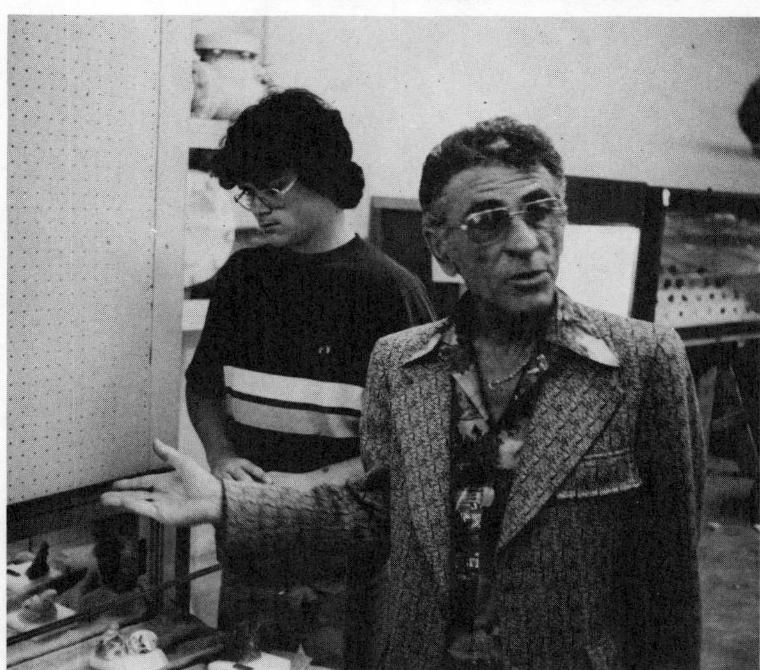

Judging of minerals, stamps, and coins will take place from 10 'til 2 in the Main Exhibit Hall. These valued collections will be available for viewing throughout the day.

No fairgoer need ever go hungry, not with the variety of food available on the grounds. . .

This year we also have several international menus to choose from. No matter where you go, you're sure to find something to please your palate.

Young riders compete in many different classes and events for local and regional honors at the Junior Horse Show which continues until 4 p.m. in the Horse Show Arena.

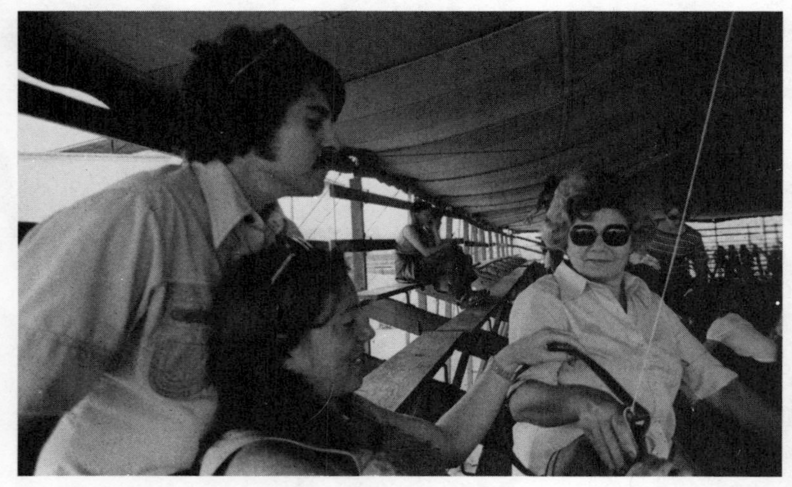

For those of you who don't own horses, you can take your child on the pony ride located in the livestock area next to Ring #1.

Everyone knows what a rabbit is, but did you know that a cavy is a guinea pig? Don't miss our expanded Rabbits and Cavies Show in Livestock Building #4.

Ray

Hundreds of barnyard fowl can now be seen in competition at the Poultry Building where FFA and 4-H members proudly display the many varieties of chickens, pigeons, turkeys, ducks, and geese they have raised.

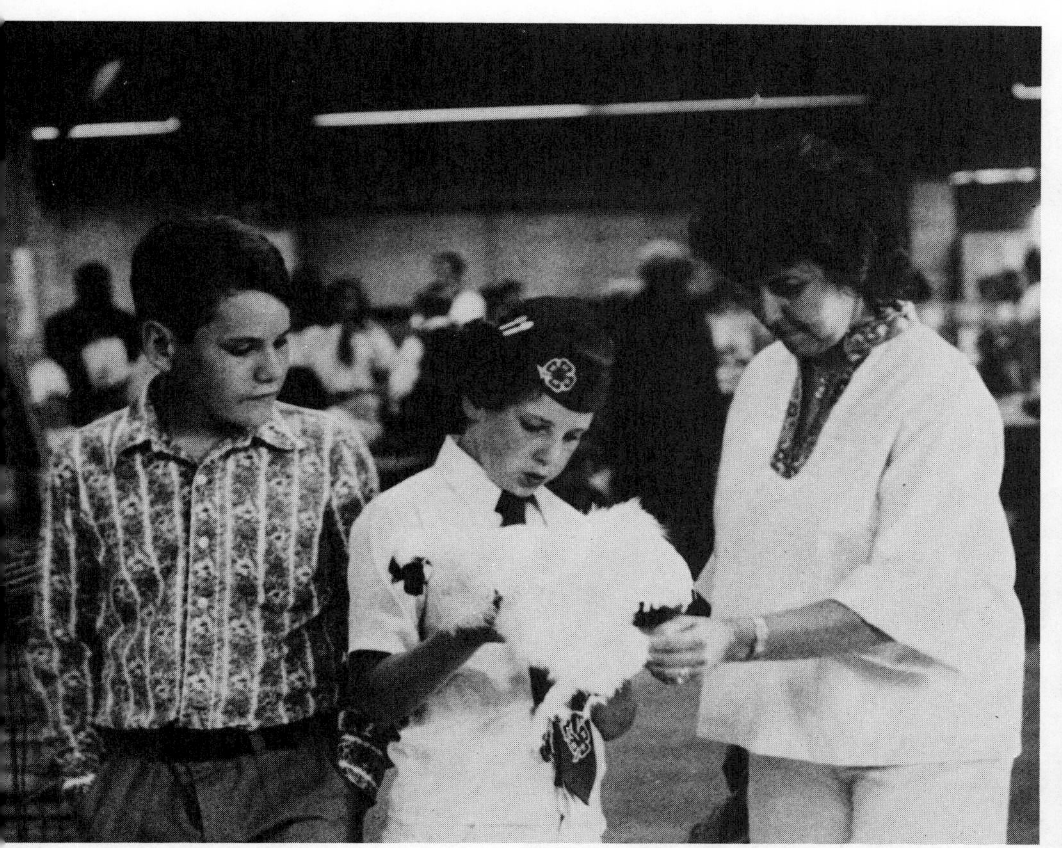

At 11 a.m. you'll be able to cheer on your favorite rooster at the always entertaining Cock Crowing Contest in Ring #1.

Tomorrow is Kid's Day. Children twelve years of age and under will be admitted free to the fairgrounds. It's an inexpensive way to enjoy a family outing.

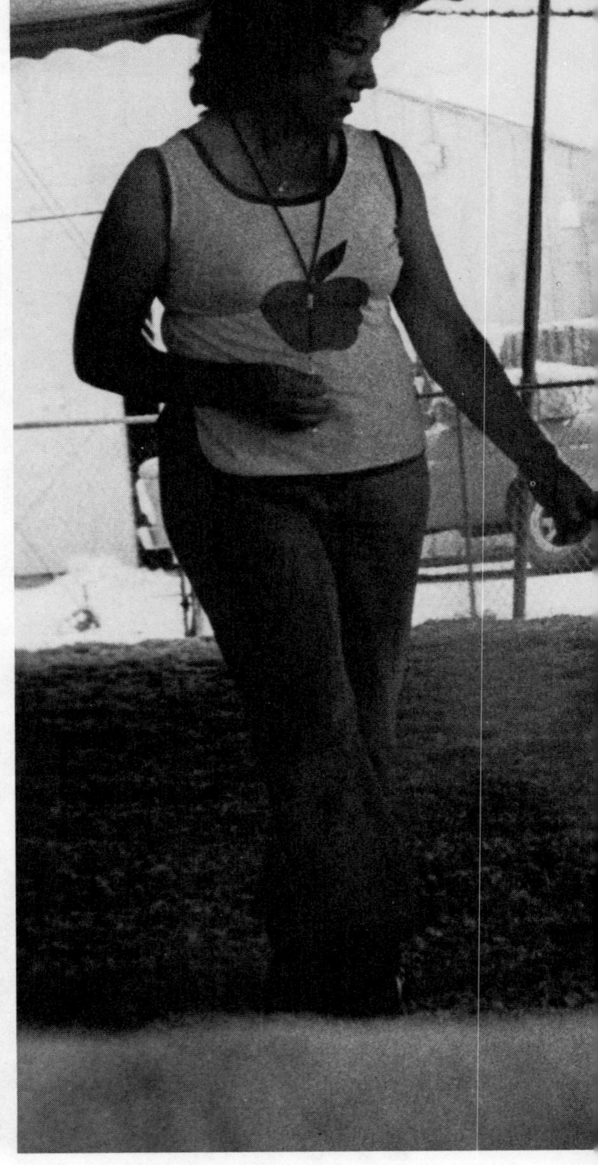

Following the Cock Crowing Contest, there will be a Sheep Dog Exhibition, also in Ring #1. It's an exciting display of a dog's ability to herd sheep at its master's command.

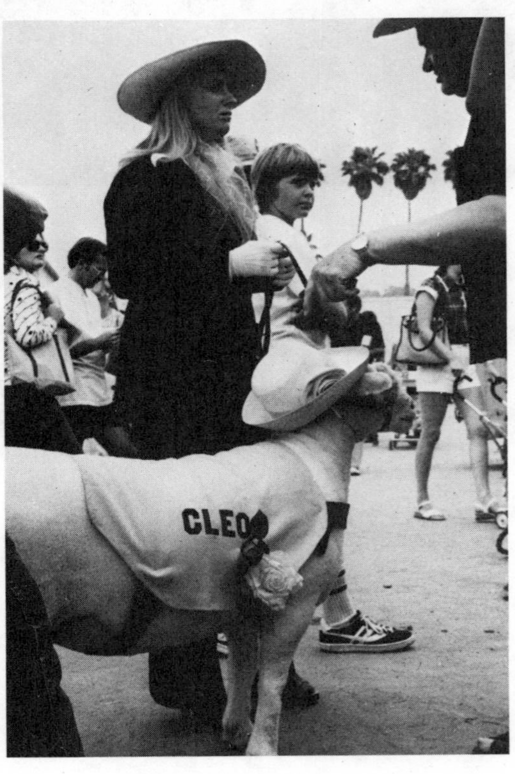

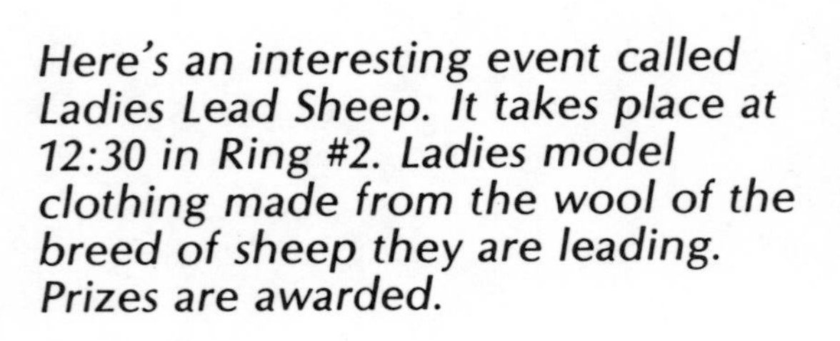

Here's an interesting event called Ladies Lead Sheep. It takes place at 12:30 in Ring #2. Ladies model clothing made from the wool of the breed of sheep they are leading. Prizes are awarded.

The championship crawl-off of the Diaper Derby begins at 1 p.m. on the Community Stage. Entrants are all less than a year old and must go the fifteen-foot distance without standing up to win, place, or show.

Tomorrow is also Photo Shoot Day. Fairgoers are invited to photograph fair attractions. Winners will be awarded trophies and other prizes on closing day.

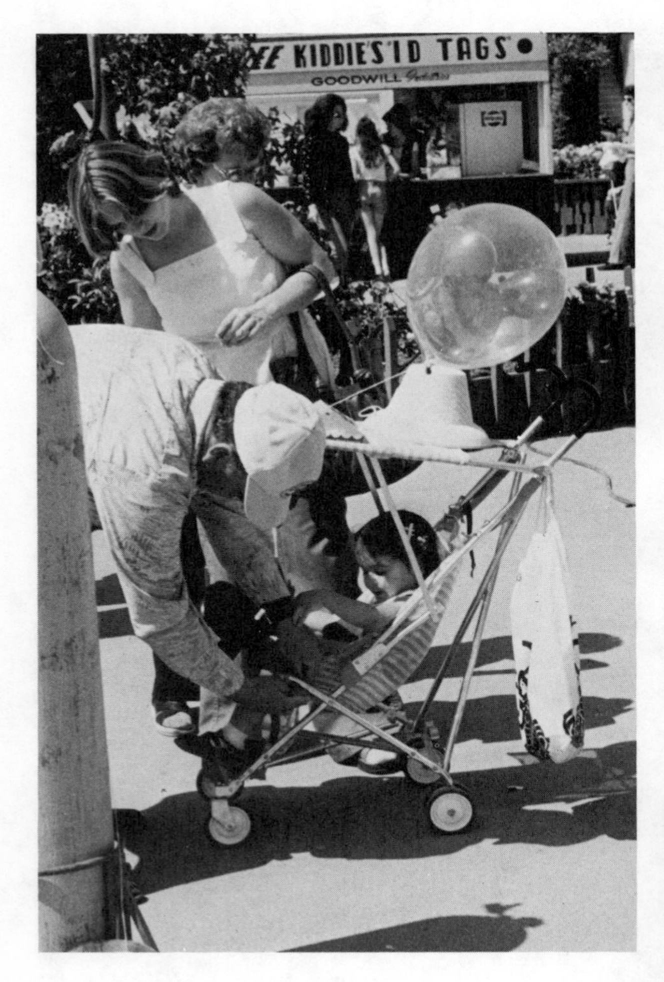

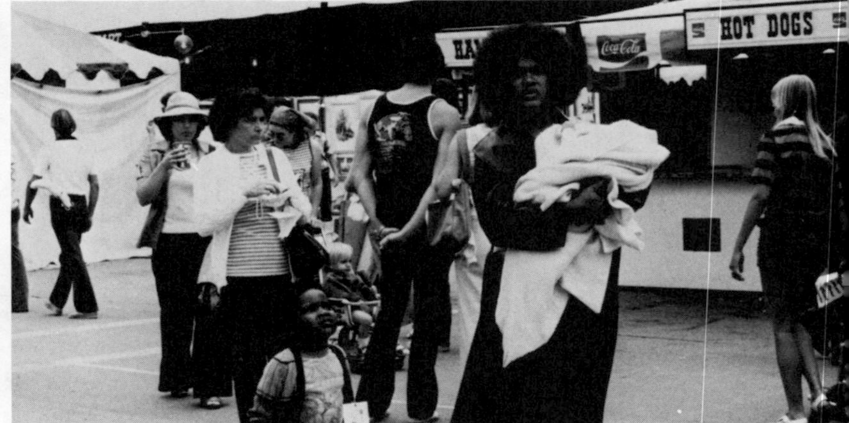

Harry Hofmann, please contact Jeannette in the Main Exhibit Hall.

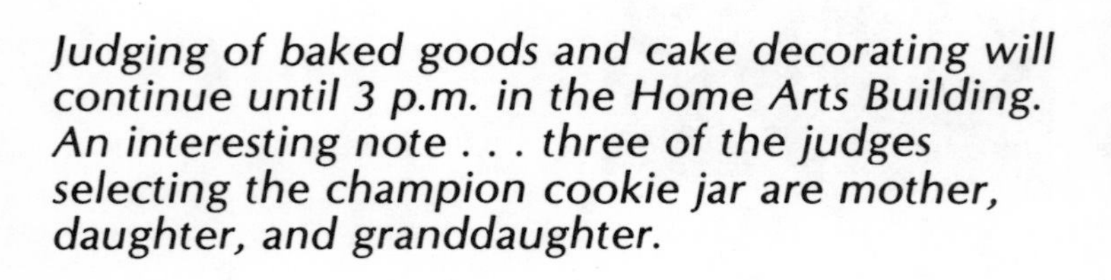

Judging of baked goods and cake decorating will continue until 3 p.m. in the Home Arts Building. An interesting note . . . three of the judges selecting the champion cookie jar are mother, daughter, and granddaughter.

Homemade pies and cakes are good for one admission each to the fair today provided they are entered in the Baked Goods Competition. Brownies are okay, too.

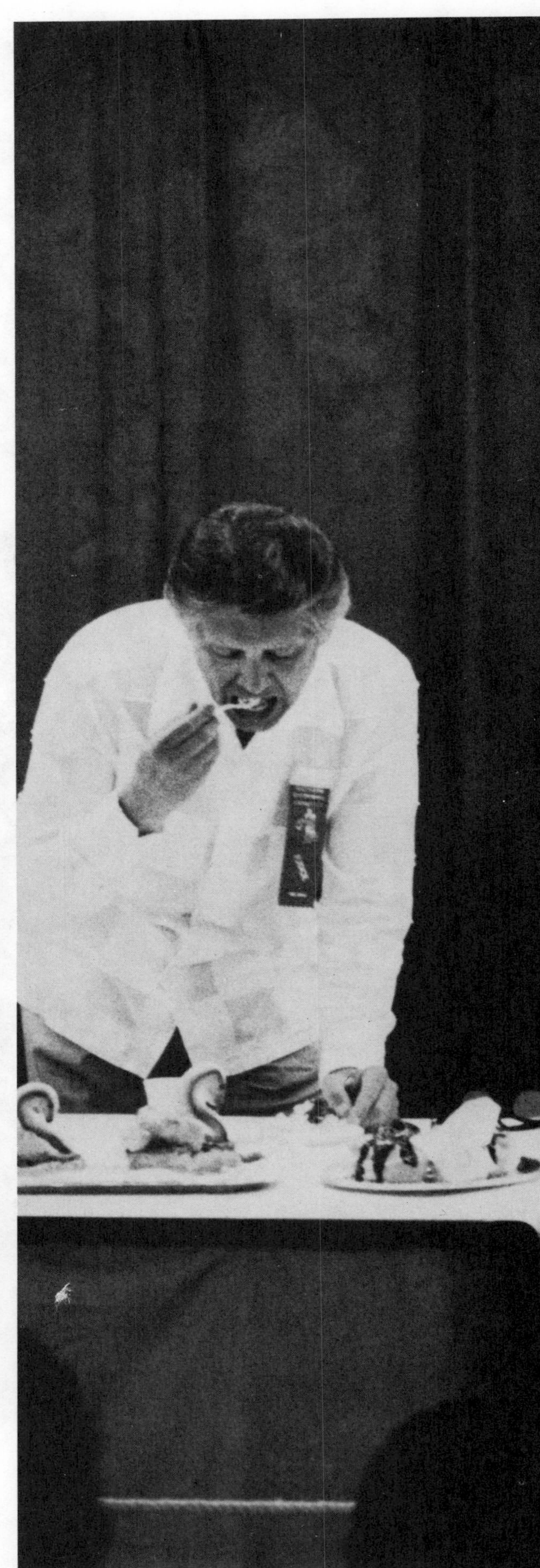

Culinary experts are invited to present their specialties for judging in the Gourmet Foods Competition this afternoon at 1 p.m., also in Home Arts.

For your safety, skateboarding is not allowed on the fairgrounds and all dogs must be on leashes.

The Cow Chip Throwing Contest will take place this afternoon at 2:30 in front of the Grandstand. All fairgoers are invited to compete for the trophy awarded for the longest toss.

See popular farm animals at the Junior and Senior Livestock Show. All cattle, sheep, goats, and swine were raised locally.

Many of the animals exhibited here at the fair are for sale. Fairgoers are welcome to meet with livestock owners for further information.

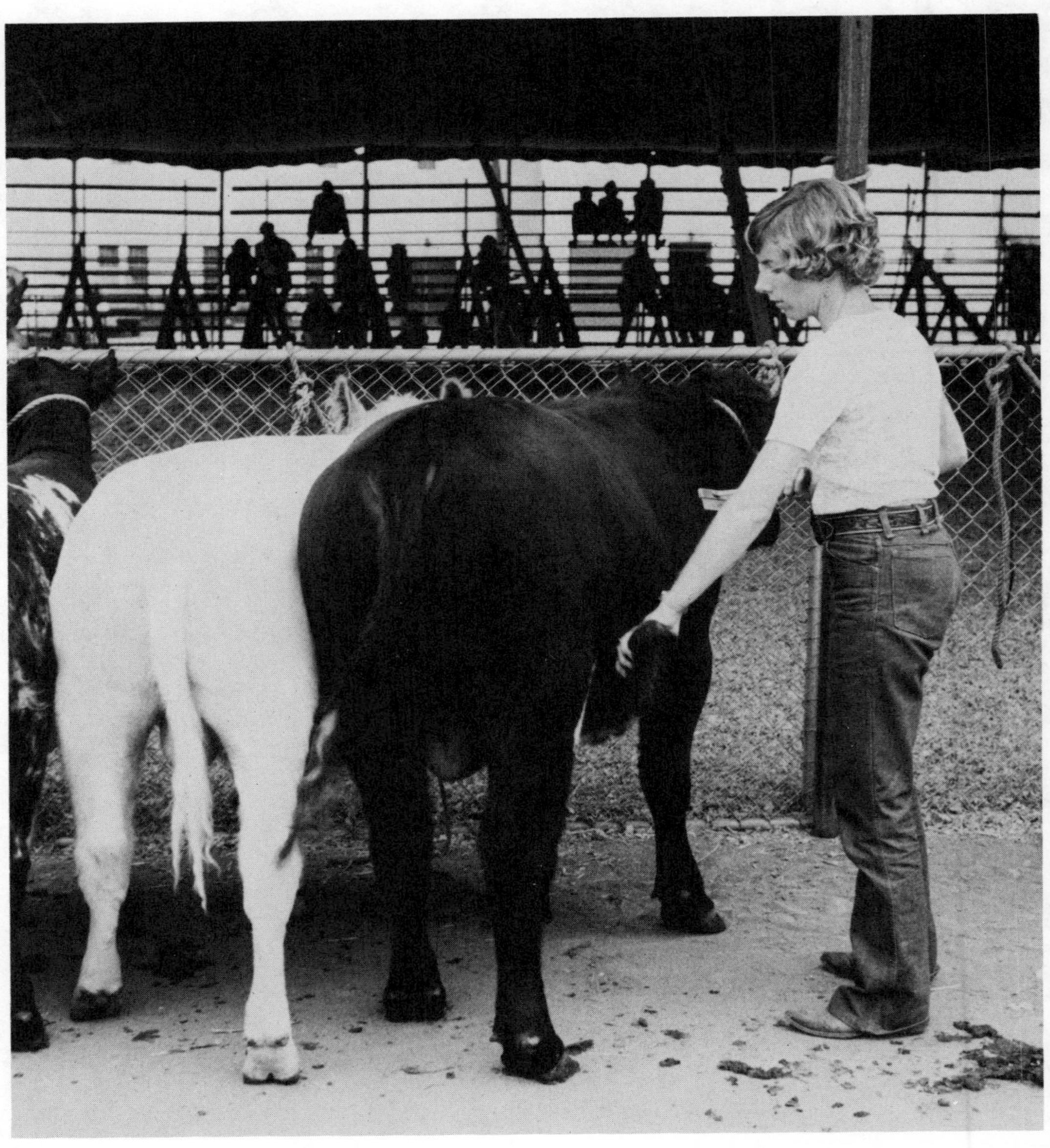

A milking demonstration will be presented daily at 2:45 in the Model Dairy Building.

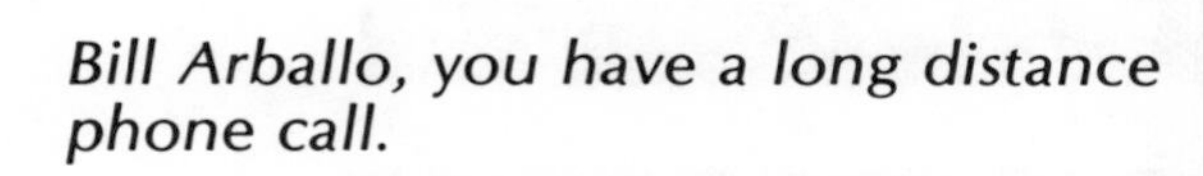

Bill Arballo, you have a long distance phone call.

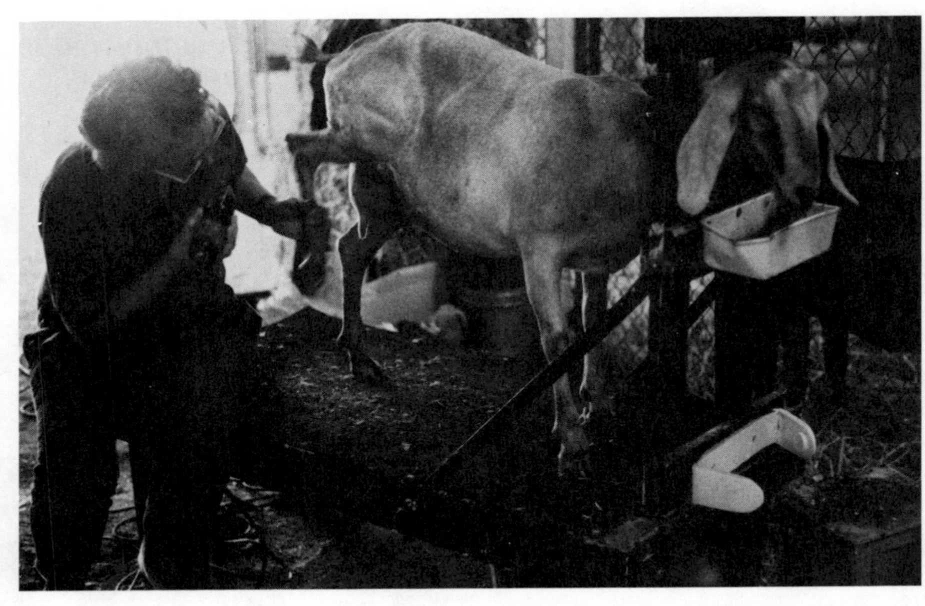

Dairy goat judging will begin in ten minutes in Ring #2.

RAMONA

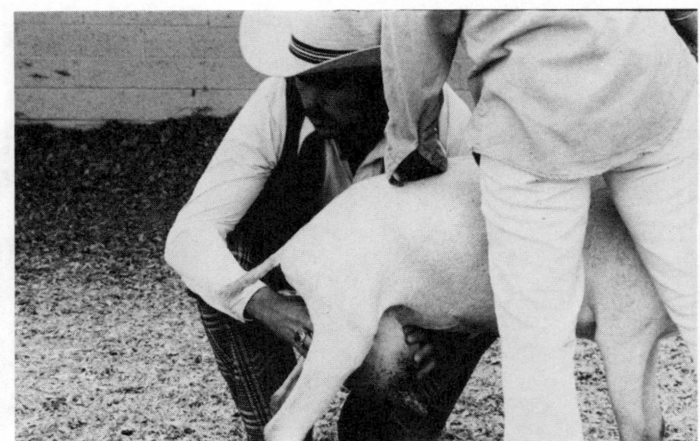

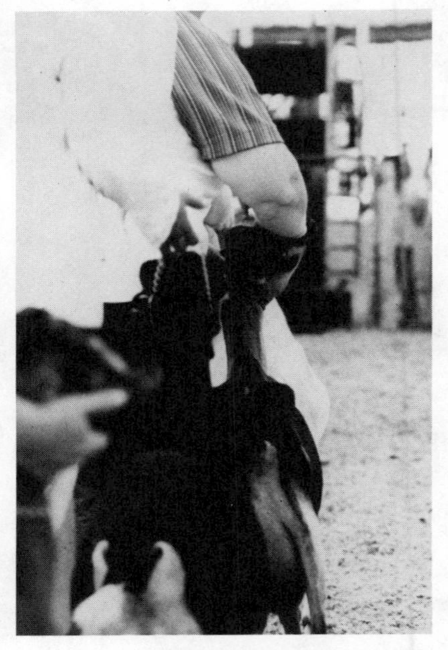

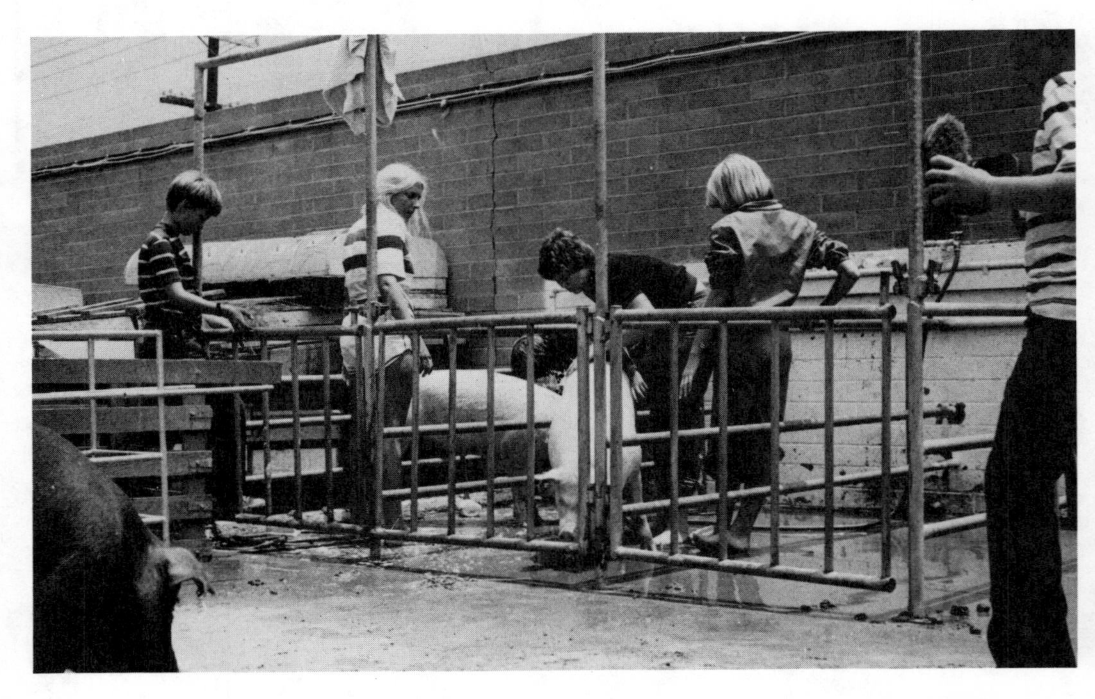

The swine and sheep competitions are two of the most popular of our livestock categories. This year we have twice as many entries in each event as last year. These animals are on display in Livestock Buildings #2 and #3.

Final judging of swine will be held in Ring #4 this afternoon at 3 p.m.

Blue ribbon winners of all cattle, sheep, and swine Junior competitions will be auctioned off to the highest bidders at the Junior Livestock Auction which begins today at 3:30 in Ring #3. This auction is one of the principal means of financing FFA and 4-H Club projects, so come early and bid high.

78 head of beef, 209 lambs, and 136 hogs are scheduled to go on the auction block this week. Last year's event raised over $178,000. Did you know that many credit cards can be used to purchase animals at the Junior Livestock Auction?

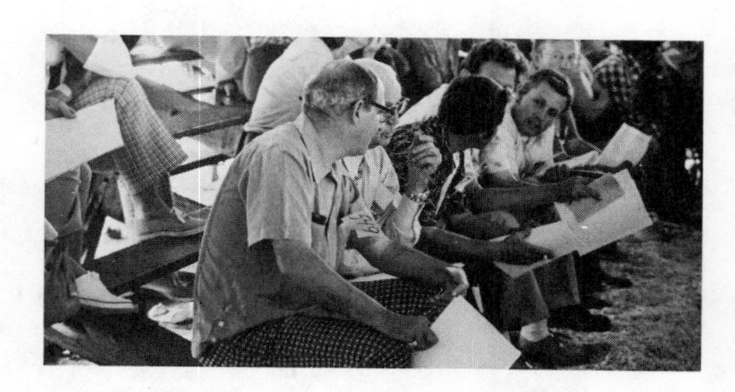

BUYER'S
ONLY

Fast and furious rodeo action continues all afternoon and it's free to every fairgoer. Don't miss the excitement! Take in a little of the Wild West as it happens in the corral area.

Today's rodeo competition includes the ladies' barrel race as well as bucking bronco and Brahma bull riding.

5

Will the parents of Diaper Derby winner Leslie Ann Miller please come to the Fair Office? We have your trophy.

FETY FILM 5063
→1A

KODAK SAFETY FILM 5063

→2

→2A

→3

FILM 5063
KODAK
→4A
→5

KODAK SAFETY FILM 506
3A

ETY FILM 5063
5A
6

KODAK SAFETY FILM 5063
6A
7

TIME
9
10
12

Don't miss this one, it's the Great Balloon Race. The centuries-old sport of ballooning will be featured this afternoon as ten hot air balloons take part in a traditional "hare and hounds chase". Takeoff is at 3 p.m. from the racetrack infield. Following that will be a thrilling parachute demonstration by the world famous U.S. Army Golden Knights.

People of all ages enjoy petting baby animals, so take the whole family to Grandpa's Barnyard. It's right next to the Model Dairy Building.

Dancing exhibitions are always a popular attraction at any fair. Many different kinds of dances are being performed here today. In the next few minutes, you can see aerobic dancing, an enjoyable form of dance exercise, on the Community Stage and Hawaiian dancing by our senior ladies on the Flower Show Stage.

An all day Square Dance Jubilee is scheduled from 9 a.m. to 5 p.m. tomorrow. All fairgoers are invited to participate in the fun.

There will be a special program today at 3:30 featuring traditional American Indian music and dance, highlighted by the appearance of Miss Indian America.

Young aspiring ballerinas representing local ballet schools will perform on the Community Stage at 4 p.m.

For those of you who find yourselves loaded down with purchases and arcade winnings, there is a checkstand near the main entrance where items may be safely held until you're ready to leave.

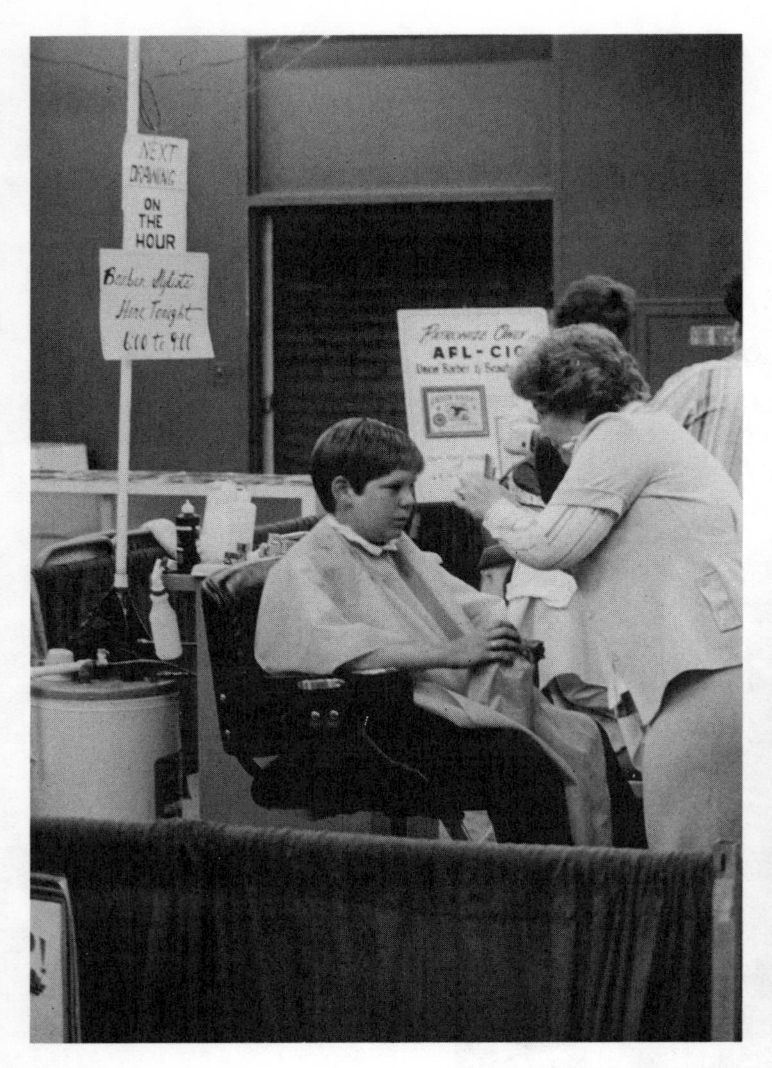

A series of demonstrations are being given in the Apprenticeship Building, including cake decorating, hairstyling, bricklaying, and electrical work.

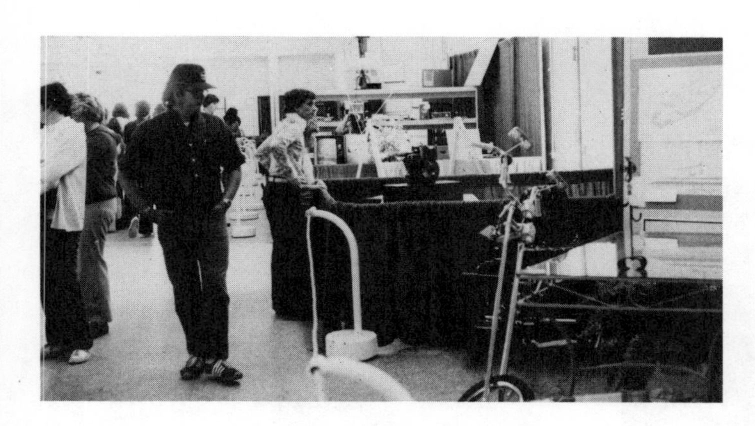

County public school students display scientific and industrial projects in the Industrial Education Building.

The next free solar energy demonstration will begin in five minutes at the Gas and Electric Display in the Main Exhibit Hall.

Persons interested in recreational vehicles can see the latest models in the Transportation Exhibit located next to the Main Exhibit Hall.

HOROSCOPE
75
HOROSCOPE

IT'S A MIRACLE..
OVER 800 YRS. OLD !
..FLESH STILL REMAINS ON MOST OF THE BODY
It's a MIRACLE
HE IS OVER 800 YRS. OLD!
ON THE BODY.
Guaranteed!
ATTRACTION.

FOR ALL AGES
FOOL THE GUESSER
HOME STATE

The whole family will enjoy the thrills and chills of our ever popular Fun Zone. And this year, it's bigger and better than ever.

ON A STICK
POP CORN
KANDY APPLES
SNO KONES

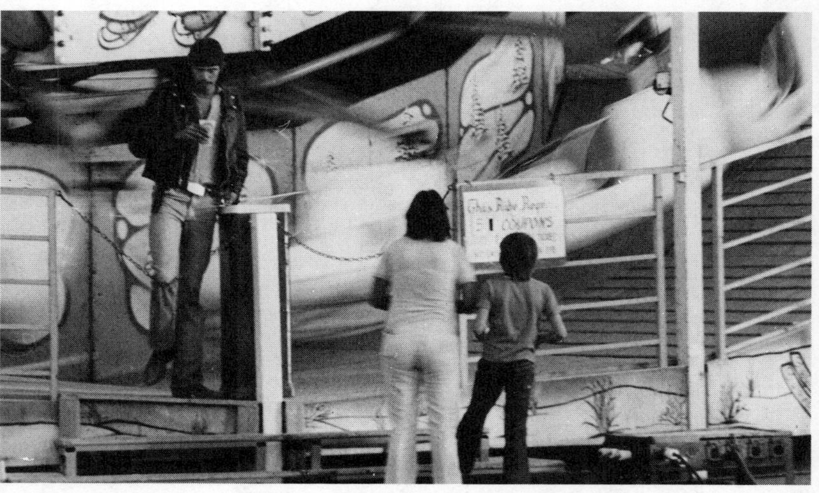

25¢

2 Coupons

15

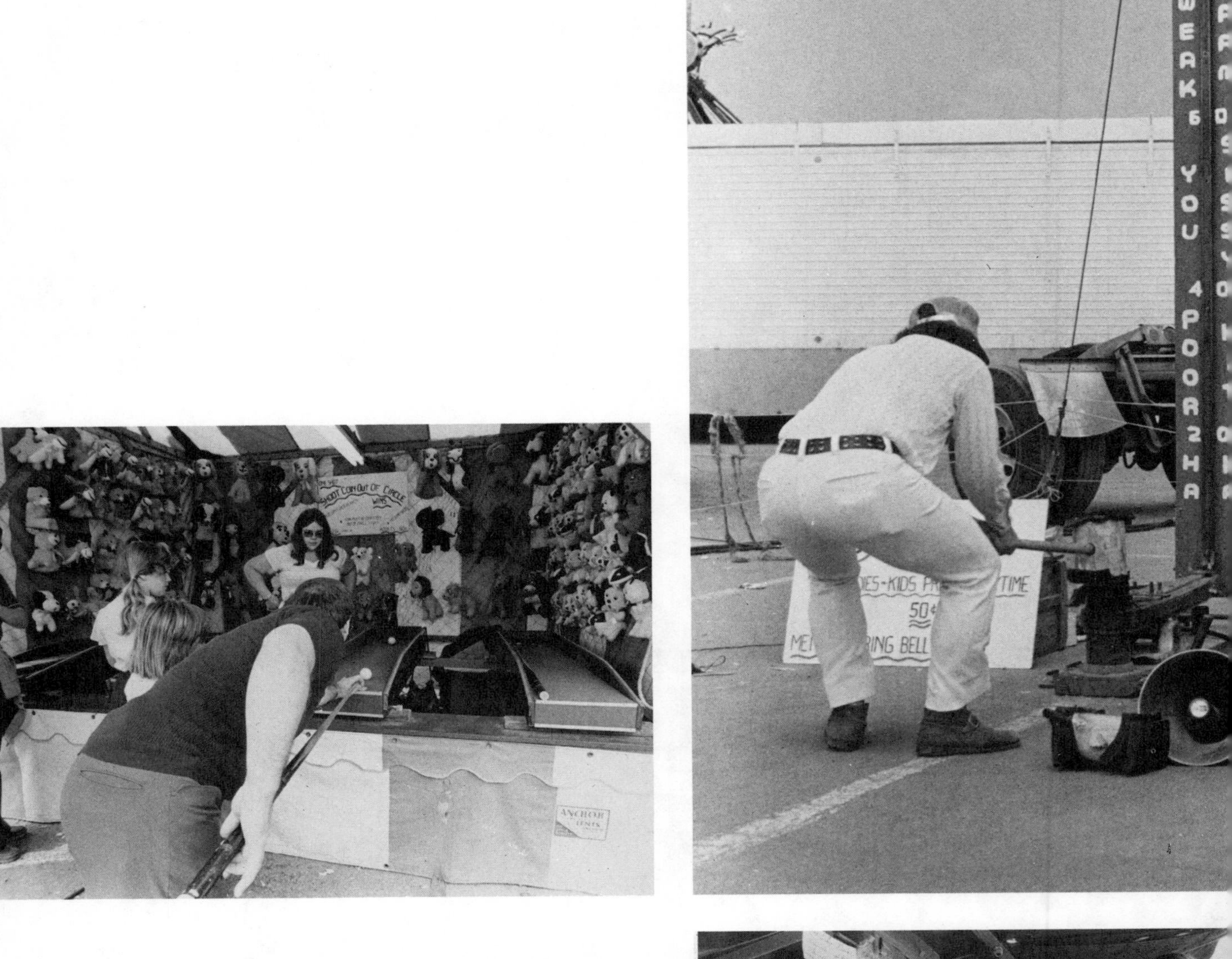

10
BAD
8
WEAK
6
YOU
4
POOR
2
HA

Test your skills and maybe win that big stuffed animal you've been wanting in the Arcade. Good luck!

ICE CREAM

The U.S. Forestry Service is now giving away 10,000 little trees at their exhibit in Building #4. . . Sorry, I mean behind Building #4.

Senior Citizens receive a special discount today on admission to the fair and at many of the concessions. We'd like to take this opportunity to welcome them and to remind you that the Senior Citizens' Talent Show will begin in fifteen minutes on the Community Stage.

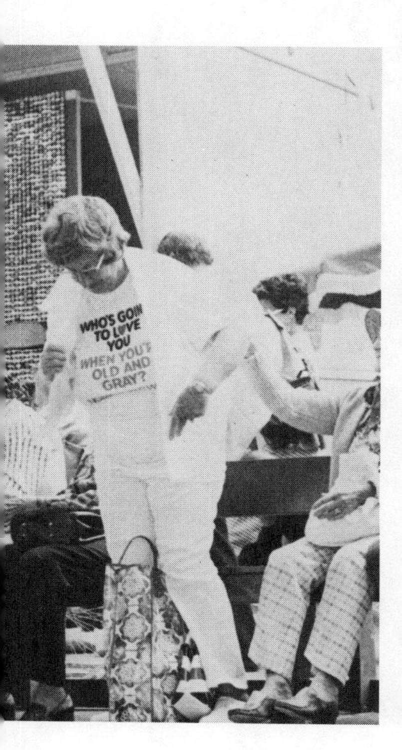
WHO'S GOIN
TO LOVE
YOU
WHEN YOU'
OLD AND
GRAY?

Bill Dumond, please come to the Grandstand.

Young ladies interested in serving as volunteer models for tomorrow's Photo Shoot activities are invited to sign up at the Special Events Office by 5 p.m.

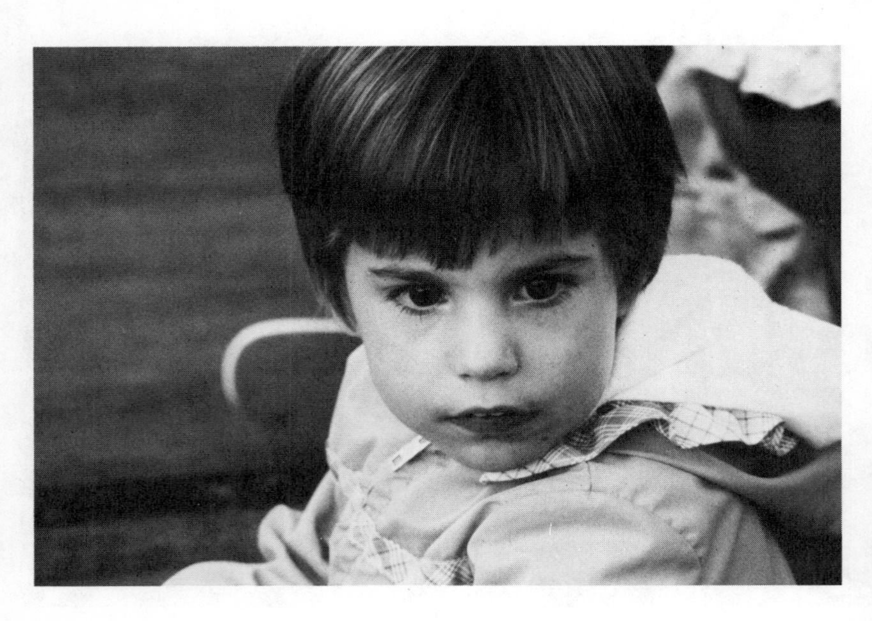

7

An unusual martial arts demonstration will take place on the Flower Show Stage at 4:15. Directly following that will be a performance by the Modern Creative Dancers.

THE
FARMER
FEEDS
AMERICA

SANDWICHES
GET A

Feature agriculture exhibits can be seen in the Main Exhibit Hall. While you're there, you can also have your blood pressure checked, register to vote, and learn some simple ways to conserve energy.

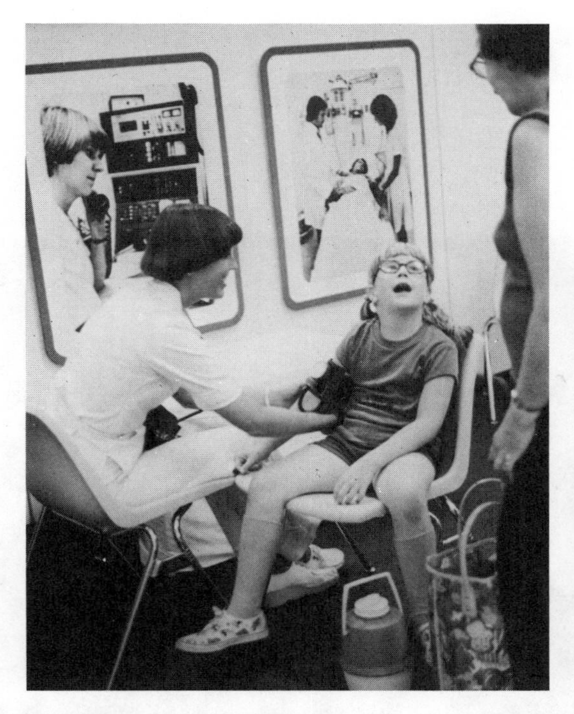

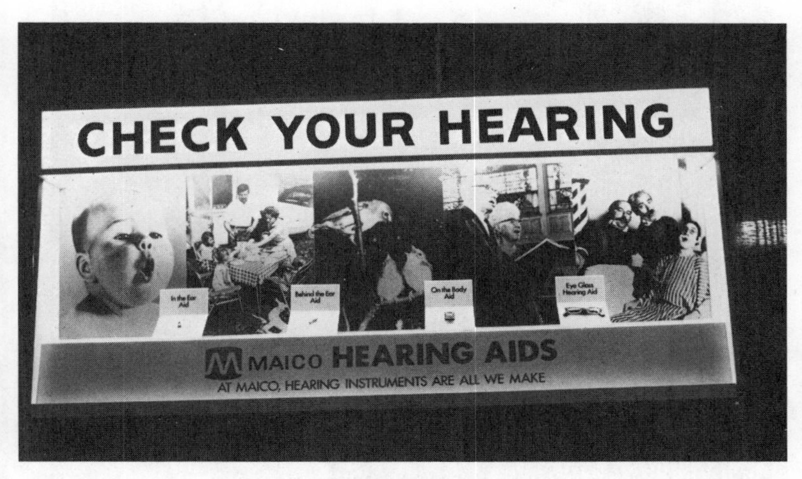

Be sure to stop by the Trade Mart and see the many new and useful products available during the fair at special reduced prices..

Remember . . . many of the products you see at the Trade Mart cannot be purchased anywhere else at any price.

For your convenience, the Postal Service trailer is located under the clock tower.

ROLL-O-MAT

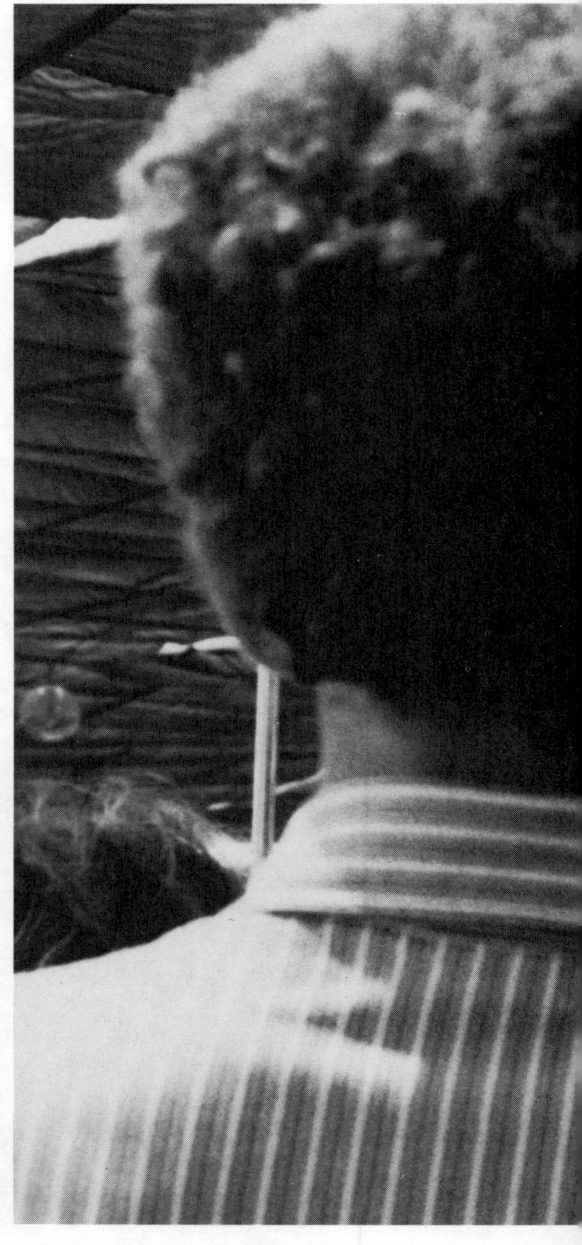

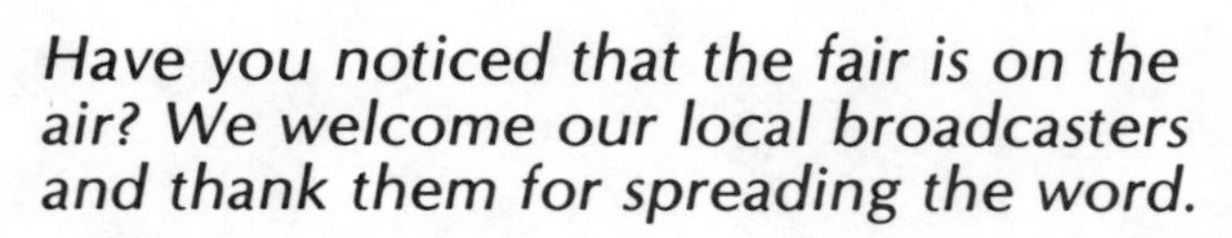

Have you noticed that the fair is on the air? We welcome our local broadcasters and thank them for spreading the word.

Persons wishing to make special arrangements for group admissions to the fair should contact Jo Jordan in the Fair Office.

SOUVENIRS

ORANGE JULIUS
"A Devilish Good Drink"
BAR B Q HOT DOGS
EDUCATION

No 1
No 2
No 3
No 4
FRENCH

Junior livestock exhibitors will show off the "best of the fair" swine, sheep, and beef animals tomorrow evening in the Parade of Grand and Reserve Champions.

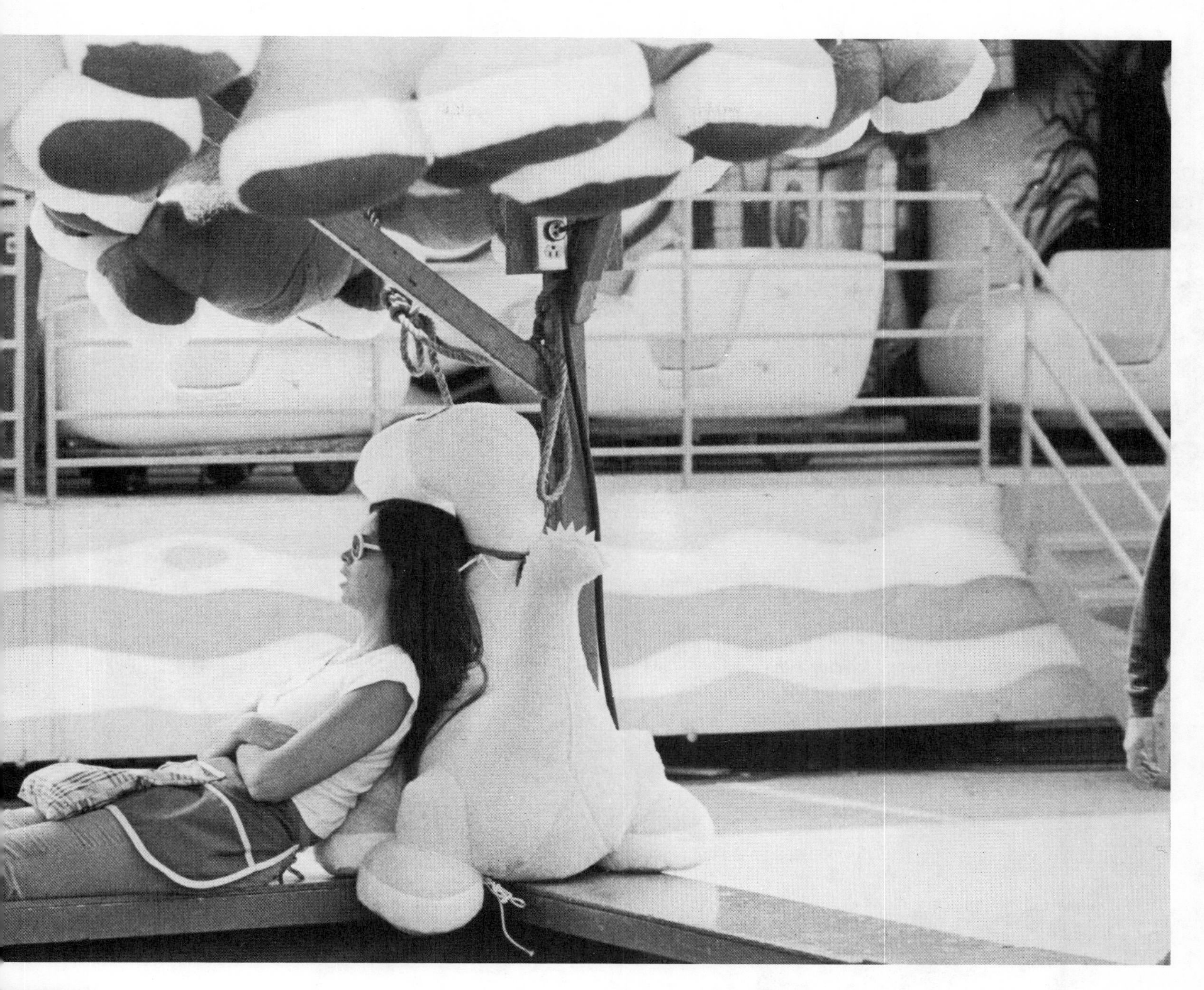

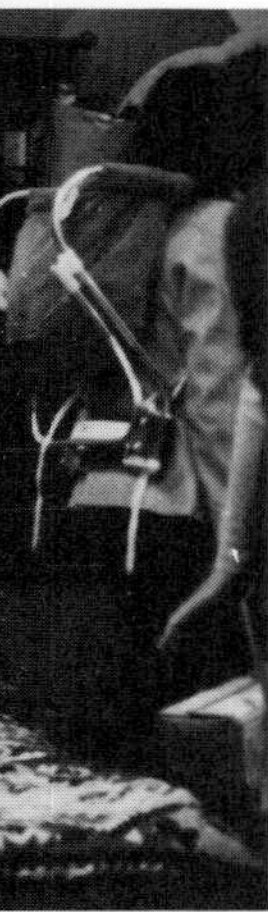

Remember. . . there will be free entertainment on the Grandstand Stage this evening as well as throughout the fair. We hope you'll stay around to enjoy the beauty of our fair at night.

Parents, do you know where your children are? If not, check the Lost Child Station at the rear of the Grandstand.

SHACK

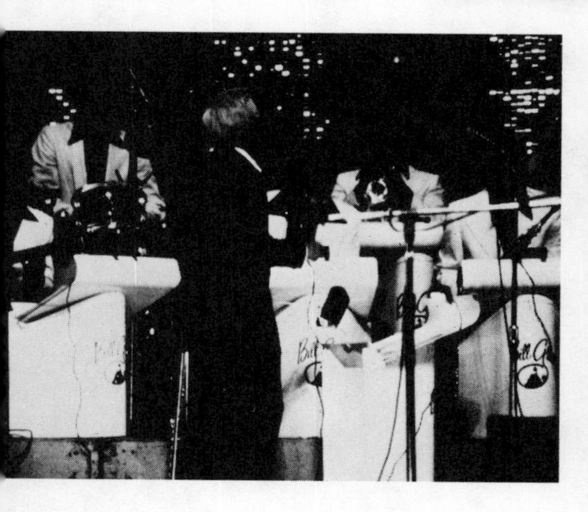

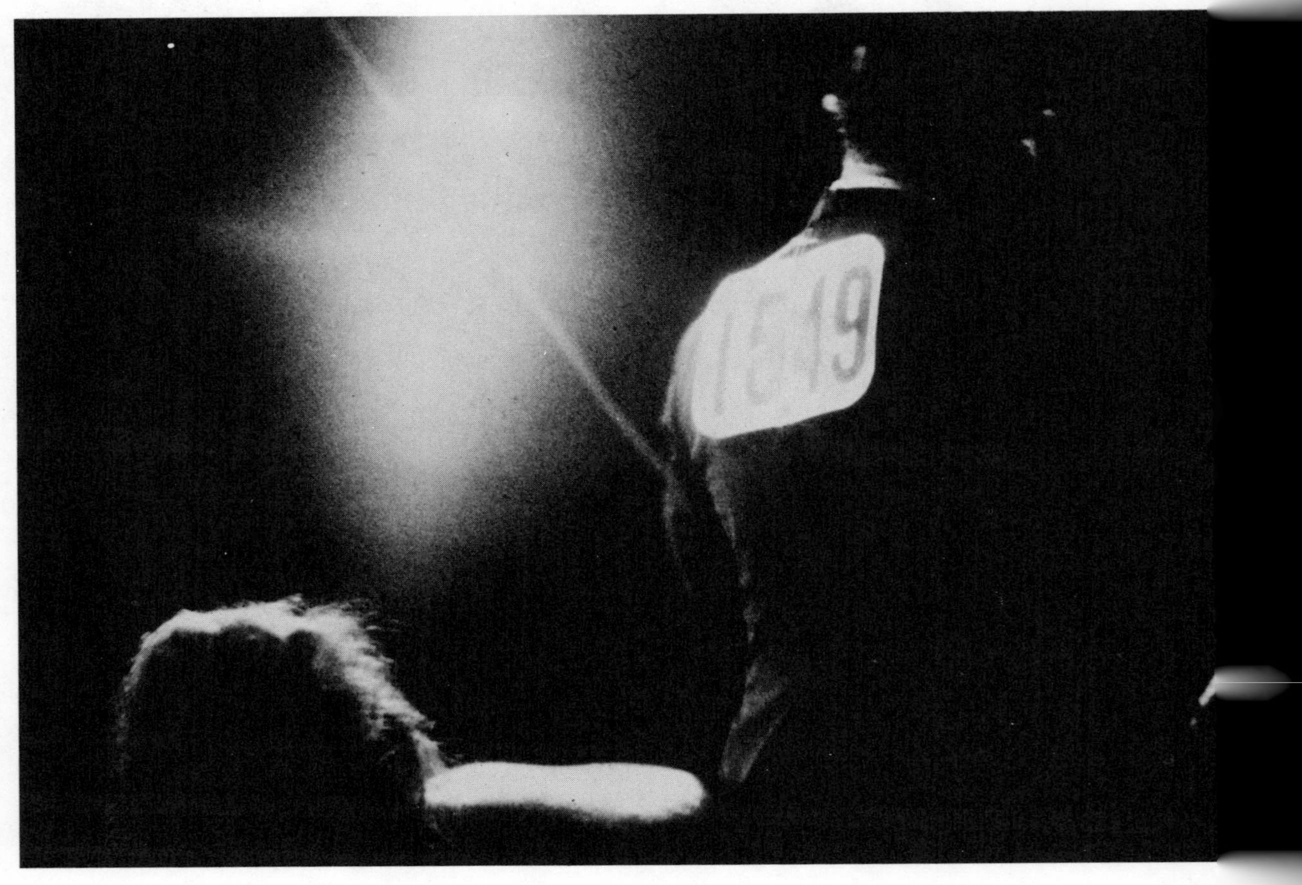

Senior Horse Show competition continues in the Horse Show Arena until 9 p.m.

Beautiful girls from throughout the county compete tonight for the coveted title of Fairest of the Fair. The lucky lady and her court, who symbolize the youthful spirit of our fair, will represent us all in the coming year.

FAIR FINALS

Tonight's free grandstand entertainment begins at 7 p.m. Your host will be Tommy Hernandez, an international film star who is better known locally as our fair's traditional goodwill ambassador, Don Diego.

This year's top entertainment includes Jose Feliciano, Buck Owens and the Buckaroos, Glenn Ash, a special appearance by the Ballet Folklórico de Mexico, the Bill Green Orchestra, and more. Remember...the show begins at 7 p.m. and seating is first come, first served, so come early.

This will be the final announcement of the day and I'd like to personally thank all of you for coming. Whether you are a participant or a spectator, it is your enthusiasm and support that make this and other county fairs possible. Please come back as often as you can this year, next year, and the years to come. Good night. . .

GREYSCALE

BIN TRAVELER FORM

Cut By Aolida E Qty 10 Date 09/24/24

Scanned By__________ Qty______ Date_______

Scanned Batch IDs

__________ __________ __________

Notes / Exception